ALBE

This edition published by
Whitecap Books Ltd
1086 West Third Street
North Vancouver, BC
Canada V7P 3J6

Produced by
Bison Books Corp.
15 Sherwood Place
Greenwich, CT 06830
USA

ISBN 0-921061-09-9

Printed in Hong Kong

RTA

TEXT	ROBIN LANGLEY SOMMER
DESIGN	SUE ROSE
PHOTOGRAPHY	PHOTO/GRAPHICS STOCK LIBRARY

Whitecap Books
NORTH VANCOUVER, B.C. CANADA

 A Bison Book

The author and publisher would like
to thank Gillian M Goslinga for editing
this book and writing the captions.

PHOTO CREDITS

Agrapha Photo Productions: 35.

D & J Abson: 64,92,124-125,126; M Burch: 61, 65,
70-71, 94, 119; J Burridge: 16, 18-19, 85; J F Garden:
1, 118; B Herger: 15, 62-63, 68-69, 74-75, 88-89, 95,
106-107, 128; J A Kraulis: 17, 20, 21,108,109;
R W Laurilla: 31, 32-33, 72-73, 81; D Leighton: 3-6,
38, 44-45, 52(top), 54-55, 58-59, 90-91; G Lunney:
76-77, 96-97; G Marx: 26-27, 66, 75, 84, 86, 91;
G E Maurer: 93; P McGinley: 80-81; Morning Star Inc:
30, 99, 116-117; S Short: 53; J Vogt: 114-115, 117,
120-121, 122; T Willis: 67(bottom); R Wright: 23, 34,
48, 79; C Young: 28-29, 37, 39, 40-41, 42, 43, 46, 47,
49, 50, 51, 52(bottom), 56, 57, 67(top), 78, 82-83, 87,
100-101, 102, 103, 104-105, 110-111, 112, 113, 123, 127.

Triple Five Corporation Ltd: 24, 25(both).

1 The wild rose is Alberta's floral emblem.

3-6 With the return of spring, the cold blue waters
of Bow River, Banff National Park, re-emerge from
beneath their thick mantle of winter ice.

INTRODUCTION

Canada's largest and most westerly prairie province is famous for the pioneer spirit that breathes through the whole history of Alberta. The adventurous voyageurs, fur traders, missionaries, 'Mounties,' cowboys and gold seekers of the early days set the pace for the energetic oilmen, ranchers, miners, builders and financiers who have been the architects of Alberta's twentieth-century prosperity. All have been affected by the province's many attractions, which include year-round sunshine due to unusually clear skies, abundant water and wildlife, incredibly rich natural resources and spectacular scenic beauties.

The province was named for Princess Louise Caroline Alberta, a daughter of Queen Victoria, who married the governor general of Canada. These two women are memorialized together in Banff National Park, where the majestic Victoria Glacier looms above emerald green Lake Louise. But before the Europeans arrived, the Indians possessed the land. In the southern prairies and foothills were the people of the Blackfoot nation, including the Blood and Piegan tribes, and their allies, the Sarcee. The Blackfoot were nomadic hunters of the plains, whose way of life was inseparable from the great buffalo herds that roamed here. The north was dominated by the Cree, a forest-dwelling people, and the Athapascan tribes.

Alberta's land area of more than 600,000 square kilometres comprises four distinct regions, each with its own kind of beauty. The far north is lightly populated and includes great tracts of virgin forest, meadows and marshes. Wood Buffalo National Park is located here, the only known nesting site of the whooping crane. Vast oil-sand reserves around Fort McMurray have brought new business and industry into northeastern Alberta in recent years, but much of the far north is still accessible only by boat or plane. The Athabasca River descends from 8100-square-kilometre Lake Athabasca, most of which is in Saskatchewan, and wends its way south and west. The Peace and Hay river systems also drain the region. The near north, closer to the provincial capital of Edmonton, is part of the huge Alberta Plain, where forests alternate with rolling prairie land. Here Lesser Slave Lake, with its wide sandy beach, forms a popular recreation area where bald eagles, moose, deer and beavers make their homes. A multitude of smaller lakes and rivers provide incomparable sport fishing for trout, northern pike, walleye and other species. Canada's smallest national park, Elk Island, is only 32 kilometres east of Edmonton, and affords a view of elk, plains bison and wood bison in their natural habitat. Other points of interest in the Edmonton area include Polar Park, Miquelon Lake, St Albert and Alberta Wildlife Park.

Edmonton itself, known as the Gateway to the North, is a dynamic modern city built along the beautiful North Saskatchewan River. The river was an important artery of the western fur trade when the Hudson's Bay Company came into the region 200 years ago. Here the first Fort Edmonton was constructed in 1795, and was soon followed by a series of other strongholds that made this region the hub of a fur-trading empire that stretched from the Rockies to Lake Athabasca. More permanent settlement began after the trading companies sold their vast holdings to the Canadian government during the 1870s. Then sawmills sprang up along the river's banks, and steamboats and sternwheelers plied its waters.

Fast-growing Edmonton had every reason to expect that the Canadian Pacific Railway would take the nearby Yellowhead Pass route through the Rockies as construction marched westward in the early 1880s—thus assuring Edmonton's future as a transportation center. But these hopes were dashed by selection of the Kicking Horse Pass route farther south, which took the railway straight through the brash young settlement of Calgary and triggered off a rivalry between the two cities that has lasted for a hundred years. However, the Canadian Northern Railway reached Strathcona, near Edmonton, in 1891, and these two communities (ultimately merged into one) became a beehive of activity, as prospectors searched the North Saskatchewan for gold. When George Carmack made his big strike in the Klondike on Bonanza Creek in 1897, Edmonton was uniquely situated to outfit the steady stream of gold seekers that surged into the north along the historic all-Canadian route to Lake Athabasca. In the early 1900s, eager pioneers were rapidly settling the great agricultural region surrounding the city, which was incorporated in 1904. The following year, Edmonton was designated the capital of the new Province of Alberta—much to the dismay of Calgary. Prosperity increased during World War II, when Edmonton became an aviation center for flights to the Arctic and thence to the Orient.

In 1947 the discovery of oil at Leduc No 1, just south of the city, generated new excitement, and other major strikes soon surrounded Edmonton with producing oil fields that secured its future as the administrative service center for the province's petrochemical industries. Today Edmonton has achieved a prominence undreamed of by its first hardy settlers, and civic pride greets one at every turn in the form of spacious modern buildings, well-tended parks and recreation centers, cosmopolitan hotels and restaurants and the $84 million Convention Center that houses Canada's Aviation Hall of Fame.

Calgary, south of Edmonton and east of the Rockies, sprang up to serve as the transportation hub for the ranching industry that began in the 1880s, when Montana cattlemen drove their herds across the Canadian border to the rich pasture lands of southern Alberta. Later Calgary would evolve into the financial center of the petroleum industry. In the beginning, though, it was a fort for the North West Mounted Police. They came into the region in the 1870s to subdue the lawlessness provoked by an influx of American whiskey traders and wolf hunters from Montana, who created unrest among the Indians. The native Blackfoot were undergoing traumatic changes to their old way of life in the face of white immigration and the decline of the buffalo herds, and the traders plied them with cheap liquor in exchange for buffalo robes. The unscrupulous wolf hunters also stirred up ill will and conflict among the native peoples until the newly formed NWMP made its advent in 1874, under Assistant Commissioner J F Macleod, and imposed order. Finally, the Blackfoot bowed to the inevitable and surrendered their ancestral lands to the government in 1877.

In the following decade, the Canadian Pacific Railroad, under the leadership of William Van Horne, forged a path across Alberta and through the Rocky Mountains to British Columbia, Canada's Pacific province. The selection by the Canadian Pacific Railway of the Kicking Horse Pass route ensured that the tiny village of Calgary would prosper. Other new towns rose rapidly along the tracks, including Medicine Hat, where Alberta's vast resources of natural gas were first discovered. Van Horne was quick to see the potential of the Rockies as a resort area after warm sulphur springs were discovered in Banff, and he vowed to "bring the people to the mountains." Calgary was a prime beneficiary of this foresight, as traffic increased from year to year. The great oil discoveries in nearby Turner Valley from 1914 onward pushed the former prairie cowtown into prominence soon after it staged the first of the great Wild West shows that would become the world-famous Calgary Stampede.

Since World War II, Calgary has been one of the fastest-growing cities in Canada and an international center for energy and finance. Called "the Bay Street of western Canada" for the many banks and businesses that occupy its gleaming high-rise buildings, it is surrounded on all sides by grain fields, ranchlands and oil wells. Calgary holds fast to its frontier heritage despite its modernity, and white Stetson hats and cowboy boots are everyday dress, even with a conservative gray flannel suit.

Travel to Alberta's beautiful Rockies is a booming industry that attracts more and more visitors each year. Kananaskis Country, a new multi-purpose recreational area west of Calgary, encompasses 4000 square kilometres of beautiful wilderness, and also offers world-class skiing, golfing and other recreational pursuits. Just north of Kananaskis is Banff, a 6594-square-kilometre paradise recently designated a World Heritage Site by the United Nations. Canada's first national park has been a popular resort since the 1880s, when CPR surveyors discovered the warm sulphur springs near Banff townsite and William Van Horne recognized the potential of the region and helped to design the classic château that became the Banff Springs Hotel. The beautiful Bow River Valley offers innumerable activities from hiking and climbing to fishing and bathing in the famous hot springs. Further north is Lake Louise, "the gem of the Rockies," framed by Beehive and Fairview mountains, between which is the great Victoria Glacier. Château Lake Louise overlooks this splendid scene with regal serenity.

North of Banff is Jasper National Park, established in 1907 shortly before the Grand Trunk Railway drove its way through the Yellowhead Pass. The early explorers of this region left few lasting marks on the pristine landscape. Trappers, traders and miners have all come and gone without spoiling the incomparable mountain scenery or destroying the habitats of Rocky Mountain sheep, nimble mountain goats or the shrill marmots whose call gave Whistler Mountain its name. The region was made accessible by the pioneering railroaders and wisely preserved by the nation as a natural treasure. Similarly, Waterton Lakes National Park, where prairies and mountains meet in Alberta's southwest, was set aside in 1895 and united with Montana's Glacier National Park in 1932 to form the world's first international peace park.

Central and southern Alberta are part of the province's vast interior plain and run from the foothills of the Rockies to the border with Saskatchewan. During the age of the dinosaurs, the region's eastern Badlands were formed by the uplifting of softer rock and periodic incursions of the sea. Some of the world's most important dinosaur-fossil discoveries have been made in central Alberta, around Drumheller and along the Red Deer Valley. In this part of the province, the semi-arid prairie of the south gives way to the fertile black soil of the Parklands, which has made this a major wheat and cattle raising district for over a hundred years. Farmers and ranchers from eastern Canada, the United States and eastern and central Europe all helped to settle the region during the late nineteenth century, when the railroads came in to supply the homesteaders and take their products to market. Alberta's Indian heritage is preserved at the Stoney Indian Reserve west of Calgary, the Blackfoot Museum at Gleichen, and Blackfoot Crossing, the gravesite of Crowfoot, last of the great Plains Indian chiefs. In Okotoks in the foothills country, an 18,000-ton boulder deposited by the glaciers bears pictographs depicting ancient Indian rites. Recreational lakes and rivers abound in this historic area, which also has many stands of timber and numerous fish and game animals.

Albertans are a friendly and hardy people, proud of their heritage and their land. Enterprising and unpretentious, they have everywhere created a good life for themselves, and are forever tapping the unlimited potential of their province, in true pioneer fashion. Whether it be the excitement of West Edmonton Mall or the serenity of the wilderness at Wood Buffalo Park, the emerald waters of Lake Louise or the bizarre hoodoo formations of the Badlands, great summer weather or excellent skiing conditions, Alberta shares something with all.

Robin Langley Sommer

EDMONTON AND THE NORTH

Edmonton's prominence is based on its dual role as the capital of Alberta and supply center for the northern part of the province. When the first Europeans arrived in the Alberta region, the south was dominated by tribes of the powerful Blackfoot nation, who ferociously resisted white incursions into the land that they had claimed for 2000 years. In the north, the Cree and the Athapascan peoples co-operated with the newcomers to what was then called Rupert's Land. The newcomers were the fur traders of the North West and Hudson's Bay companies, who built trading posts throughout the region from 1788. These two rival companies merged in 1821, and the fur trade dominated the life of northern Alberta for another 50 years.

In the late 1800s, the Grand Trunk and Canadian Northern railways opened up the vast northern plains to settlement. Thousands of homesteaders poured into the region, drawn by the promise of cheap land and the unlimited opportunities to make a new life in what would soon become Canada's westernmost prairie province. Alberta joined Confederation in 1905, with Edmonton as its capital. Nearby Strathcona became part of the city in 1912, which increased the region's vitality and importance as a traffic centre.

During World War II, Edmonton became a key base on the route to the Orient when Arctic air routes were developed. The city prospered as it had during gold-rush days, when it served as "the back door to the Klondike." At the same time, the United States constructed the Alaska Highway to counter the threat of a Japanese invasion with an overland route to Alaska, and Edmonton was headquarters for the construction work and for American service personnel. After the war, in 1947, Edmonton began its newest cycle of prosperity with the discovery of oil at Leduc No 1, just south of the city. Pembina, Woodbend and Redwater followed in quick succession, and the capital embarked on its new career as the administrative service center for Alberta's thriving petroleum industry, which had begun with the discoveries in Turner Valley 33 years earlier.

Today Edmonton is a vibrant modern city whose skyline is dominated by gleaming skyscrapers and whose population of 700,000 is much younger than the national average. The city is built along the scenic North Saskatchewan River, which is bordered by 27 kilometres of parkland linked by hiking and bicycle trails. Residents are quick to point out such landmarks as the Alberta Legislature, the Centennial Library, the Citadel Theatre and Fort Edmonton Park. The world's largest indoor playground and shopping centre is located at West Edmonton Mall, whose Ice Palace is the practise rink for the city's beloved NHL hockey team, the Oilers.

The capital provides access to the vast region known as northern Alberta, much of which is unspoiled wilderness. Prairie grasslands alternate with thick forests, beautiful lakes and rivers, and wildlife refuges like Thunder Lake Provincial Park, a nesting site for the graceful blue heron. Grizzly bears still frequent the Swan Hills region. The town of Grande Prairie is a thriving community of the northwest, servicing the agricultural, petrochemical and forest-products industries. The majestic Athabasca River and its tributaries drain all of northern and north-central Alberta and provide a waterway system to the Arctic that has been traveled since prehistoric times. High in the northeast is historic Fort Chipewyan, at the western end of Lake Athabasca, whence Alexander Mackenzie began his voyage in search of the Northwest Passage in 1789. His route to the Arctic followed the Slave River, which parallels the eastern boundary of Wood Buffalo National Park. West of the park is the fertile Peace River country.

15 A "knob and kettle" terrain interspersed with lakes makes Elk Island Park, 32 kilometres east of Edmonton, one of Canada's most beautiful wildlife sanctuaries.

16 Edmonton at night, with the imposing Alberta Legislature Building illuminated in the foreground.

17 Completed in 1912 on one of the early sites of Fort Edmonton, the Legislature Building boasts a stately cupola.

18-19 Established as a fort in 1795, Edmonton grew into a thriving pioneer community. Today, its downtown competes with the most modern of city landscapes.

20 The five glass pyramids of the Muttart
Conservatory and Horticultural Centre house
more than 700 plant species from arid, temperate
and tropical climate zones.

21 The sharp lines and futuristic architecture of
downtown buildings reflect Edmonton's ongoing
growth.

20

22 The most popular of historical recreations in Fort Edmonton Historical Park is the Hudson's Bay Company Trading Post, which was the start of present-day Edmonton.

23 Children gaze longingly at the sweets in one of the park's many historic shops, which recreate the daily lives of early Edmontonians.

24 and 25 top Sixteen stories high and covering an area of five football fields, the West Edmonton Mall houses a water park with an indoor lake featuring this authentic Spanish Galleon, four glass-bottom submarines, and a rich aquatic life.

25 bottom Visitors to the spectacular West Edmonton Mall stroll down picturesque Europa Boulevard, filled with retail stores featuring the lines of world famous international designers.

26-27 "Donkey heads" are a familiar sight in the oil-rich farmlands surrounding the city.

HUDSON'S BAY OIL & GAS
Medicine River Unit #3
CPOG MED R 12-27-39-3 W5M

28-29 *Aspen, along with balsam fir, paper birch, and spruce, is a common species in Alberta's northern forests. In fact, aspen is the first tree species to regenerate after a forest fire.*

30 *A glowing harvest moon rises over a drilling rig in the plains north of Edmonton.*

31 *Lighting the sky afire, the sun dips into the waters of Cold Lake, renowned for its excellent commercial and sport fishing of whitefish, an international delicacy. The eastern part of the lake straddles the border with Saskatchewan.*

32-33 *A solitary cabin overlooks frozen Wabamun Lake in the quiet of winter, just outside of Entwistle on the Yellowhead Highway.*

34 *Vegreville celebrates its Ukrainian heritage with an eight-by-six-metre aluminum egg sculpture.*

35 *Edmonton's popular Klondike Days festival, celebrated in July, is replete with frontier belles sporting extravagant costumes.*

CALGARY

The Calgary region was largely unknown until many years after cartographer David Thompson wintered there in 1787. Thompson was one of the few white men to successfully enter the region at a time when the Blackfoot Indians still could prevent settlements on their sacred land. Not until the late 1860s, then, did southern Alberta become the scene of hectic activity, as lawless American buffalo hunters and whiskey traders moved in to exploit the Indians. In exchange for their valuable buffalo robes, the traders offered cheap whiskey that incited violence among the Indians and led to wild shoot'em-ups at such notorious trader strongholds as Robber's Roost, Whiskey Gap and Whoop-up. In 1874 the newly formed North West Mounted Police began to restore order in the territory from their headquarters at Fort Macleod. Fort Calgary was the 'Mounties' second post, established in 1875. It was incorporated as a town in the following decade, when the Canadian Pacific Railroad came through.

The fledgling city burned to the ground in 1886, but Calgarians soon rebuilt it, choosing sandstone over wood to ensure against a second fire. Americans came into the territory with cattle herds from Montana, and English gentlemen farmers were attracted by publicity about North American cattle ranching. Soon cash-crop farming was added to the regional economy, and Calgary's population increased about 1000 percent in the first decade of the twentieth century. It was Calgary's first millionaire, meat-packer Pat Burns, who joined forces with Wild West showman Guy Weadick to stage the forerunner of the famous Calgary Stampede— "The Last and Best Great West Frontier Days Celebration" of 1912. As it turned out, that was only the beginning. Today close to a million visitors turn out to help Calgarians celebrate the Stampede during the first half of July. A massive parade precedes 10 days of competition at Stampede Park, which include bronco and bull riding, steer wrestling, calf roping and the famous Chuckwagon Races. Fireworks, casino gambling and dancing in the streets provide 24-hour-a-day entertainment during the two-week event.

Calgary's rise to world prominence in the petroleum industry began in 1914 with the discovery of oil at the well called Dingman No 1. The province's first oil refinery opened in Calgary nine years later, and subsequent discoveries fueled decades of prosperity and growth. Despite the adverse effects of economic recession and declining oil prices in the early 1980s, Calgary has pursued an optimistic and expansionist policy that won it the 1988 Winter Olympics. The city's beautiful natural setting and many park areas combine with its many other attractions to entice a burgeoning tourist trade. Year-round municipal attractions include the Calgary Tower, the Glenbow Museum, the Convention Center and the Four Seasons Hotel. Fort Calgary, Heritage Park and the Calgary Centennial Planetarium and Science Center also attest to the city's concern with both its past and its future.

37 Calgary, Canada's oil capital, is here seen at night, with the Bow River in the foreground.

*38 A charming view of Calgary's skyline from the
cool banks of Bow River in summertime.*

39 A wall of shimmering glass towers reflects the brilliance of the last light of day.

40-41 In the foreground, in sharp contrast to Calgary's downtown highrises, stands the Saddle Dome, the city's sports and entertainment arena.

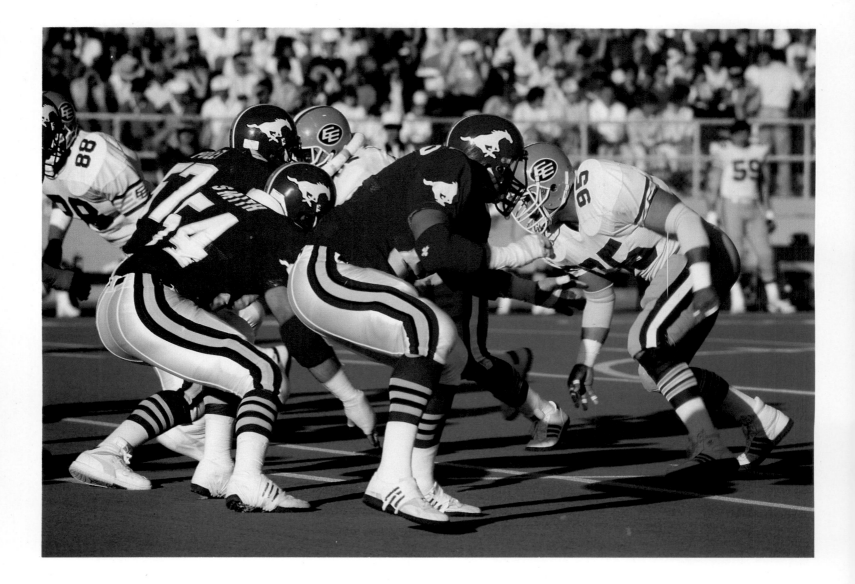

42 The rivalry between Alberta's two largest cities, Calgary and Edmonton, has always been fierce, but never as fierce as when the Calgary Stampeders play the Edmonton Eskimos.

43 Warm summer weather lends itself to outdoor
pursuits, such as this bicycle marathon.

44-45 A forest of highrises towers over the older
city, comfortably nestled at the confluence of the
Bow and Elbow rivers in an oasis of lush greenery.

C.P.R 2024

46 Calgary's Heritage Park recreates a pioneer community featuring a hotel, a general store, a ranch house, and this handsome steam locomotive, reminiscent of the early days of the Canadian Pacific Railway.

47 A young Sarcee girl, native to the region, performs in a traditional beaded costume at the Calgary Stampede, which for many is the greatest rodeo show on earth.

48 Alberta's many wilderness trails are ideal for
an adventurous and exciting day of cross country
skiing.

49 Polo players enjoy a match outside of Calgary
—a sport which points to Canada's strong
European heritage.

50 The Calgary Stampede, the largest rodeo in North America, features all the cowboy arts, including these hair-raising daily chuckwagon races.

51 Cowboy hats are a popular item for sale at the Stampede.

52 top Calgary youngsters painted this colorful and imaginative mural to beckon visitors to the 1988 Winter Olympics in Calgary.

52 bottom Heidi and Howdy, the Olympic mascots, welcome visitors to Calgary.

53 Mount Allan is the site of the 1987 World Cup Skiing competition, and part of the 1988 Winter Olympics.

54-55 The rich prairie east of Calgary offers the perfect conditions for raising thoroughbred horses.

56 The Glenmore Reservoir offers fine opportunities for sailing in Calgary.

57 Visitors have hands-on experience at the Calgary Zoo, Canada's second largest zoological park.

58-59 Calgary's most distinctive landmark is the 195-metre-high Calgary Tower, which dominates the city's skyline. The summits of the Rockies form a jagged backdrop in the distance.

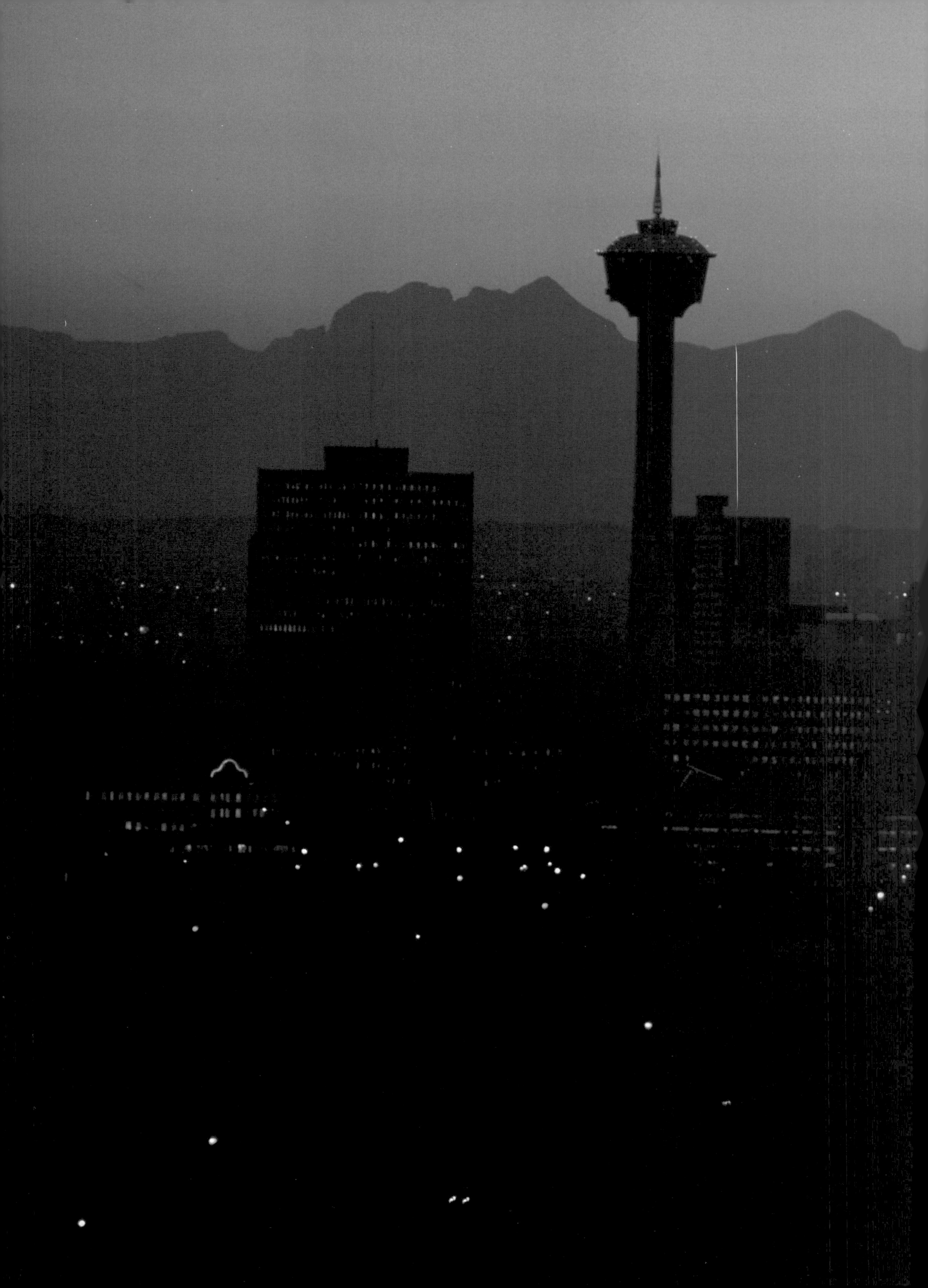

BANFF AND JASPER NATIONAL PARKS: THE CANADIAN ROCKIES

The Canadian Rockies, on Alberta's southwestern border with British Columbia, include some of the world's most breathtaking scenery. The region was created by convulsive movements within the earth almost 60 million years ago, which uplifted great masses of rock into spectacular jagged peaks. Then the Ice Age and erosion, wind and time, furrowed and carved these young mountains, clothed them in forests and meadows and threaded them with sparkling lakes and rivers.

Banff National Park comprises over 6000 square kilometres of natural beauty, including the five steep mountains that encircle Banff townsite: Rundle, Tunnel, Cascade, Norquay and Sulphur. The sheer northeast face of Mount Rundle testifies to the magnitude of the convulsions that lifted these peaks from beneath the earth. The majestic Banff Springs Hotel dominates the view from the town, and Tunnel Mountain is the scene of the popular Banff Centre Festival of the Arts, held every summer from May to August. Excellent fishing in Lake Minnewanka, Two Jack and Johnson lakes attracts sportsmen from all over. Sightseers on the Vermilion lakes Road are likely to catch glimpses of the beavers, moose and migratory birds that make their homes in the surrounding marshes. And no visit to Banff would be complete without the peerless view of Lake Louise mirroring the mountains and Victoria Glacier above it.

The Icefield Parkway between Lake Louise and Jasper townsite is an incredible journey past more than a hundred glaciers and such scenic wonders as Athabasca Falls, Bridal Veil and the immense Columbia Icefield. Peyto Lake, in the Mistaya Valley, is one of the sights that should not be missed. Its waters, dark blue in winter, turn emerald green after the spring melt, a phenomenon common to glacial lakes. Jasper townsite is at the meeting place of the Athabasca and Miette rivers, close to Whistlers Mountain, which commands a fine view of the Athabasca Valley. From the mountain one can also see Mount Robson, the highest peak in the Canadian Rockies, and Yellowhead Pass, named for the fair-haired hunter and trapper, Pierre Hatsinaton.

Pyramid and Patricia lakes, below Pyramid Mountain, are among the most popular picnic sites in Jasper National Park. Another point of notable beauty is Maligne Canyon, a dramatic limestone gorge carved by fast-running waters and cascading waterfalls. Nearby Maligne Lake, whose centrepiece is haunting Spirit Island, is one of the most-photographed vistas in the Canadian Rockies and can best be appreciated by boat. Forty-four kilometres east of Jasper townsite are the Miette Hot Springs, which offer new facilities for bathers and visitors. Everywhere in the Canadian Rockies, one finds something to delight the eye or to restore the spirit wearied by the headlong rush of daily life.

61 Because of its extraordinary emerald green waters, Lake Louise in Banff National Park is known as one of the ten natural wonders of the world.

62-63 Surrounded by breathtaking beauty, a young boy fishes in Bow Lake, Banff National park.

64 Luxuriously nestled in its wilderness setting, the world-famous Banff Springs Hotel enjoys an impressive view of Bow Valley.

65 Château Lake Louise, resplendent with summer colors, is a favorite with tourists.

66 The North American plains were once covered with a moving carpet of bison. Today the bison, one of Alberta's endangered species, is protected on reserves.

67 top The dry and open forests of the montainous areas in the Alberta Rockies are the mule deer's favored grazing grounds.

67 bottom The impressive black bear can also be spotted in the alpine forest.

68-69 Patricia Lake, in Jasper National Park, gently mirrors the autumn foliage of nearby aspens.

70-71 Castle Mountain provides a majestic backdrop for the clear waters of Bow River, Banff National Park's major waterway.

72-73 *Mount Lefroy is a hardy challenge for any mountain climber, but the reward is a dazzling panoramic view of the Rockies.*

74-75 *A solitary canoe, dwarfed by 3525-metre-high Mount Victoria, silently glides through the early mist on Lake Louise.*

75 *In winter, Athabasca Falls in Jasper National Park freezes into a fluid and magnificent sculpture of ice.*

76-77 *In an exquisite interplay of colors, the sun sets over the Canadian Rockies, Banff National Park.*

78 *Rocky Mountain bighorn sheep are easy to sight along the Icefield Parkway in Banff National Park, but not often when with young.*

79 *The surefooted Rocky Mountain bighorn ram.*

80-81 Hikers rest along the Colin Range in Jasper National Park.

81 In contrast to the crowded slopes of skiing resorts, a vast expanse of wilderness robed in white surrounds this solitary skier, a skiing experience common in the Canadian Rockies.

82-83 The 36-hole Kananaskis Golf Course has a spectacular view of mountains and plunging streams.

84 Early morning light bathes a mountain peak
in Banff National Park.

85 Dusk gently stills the pristine waters of
Maligne Lake, Jasper National Park, the world's
second largest glacial lake.

86 A brilliant rainbow graces the 22-metre plunge of Athabasca Falls in Jasper National Park.

87 Lake Louise is crowned by the regal Château Lake Louise.

88-89 The deep blue waters of Moraine Lake are chilled by winter in the Valley of the Ten Peaks.

90-91 *The rugged summit of Mount Athabasca stands at the border of Banff and Jasper national parks.*

91 *The beautiful and hardy Indian paintbrush brightens alpine meadows, where the nights remain cold even in spring and summer.*

92 An easy climb to the summit of Whistlers Mountain in Jasper National Park yields a spectacular view.

93 A favorite winter sport in the Rockies is cross-country skiing pictured here with The Ramparts, Jasper National Park, in the background.

94 A hiker stops to take in the awesome beauty of Mount Rundle and the Bow River Valley below.

95 Trail rides are popular in Paradise Valley, Banff National Park.

96-97 Glacial runoff gives Peyto Lake in Banff National Park its distinctive color.

LAND OF THE CHINOOK, FOOTHILLS AND PRAIRIES

Central and southern Alberta comprise the foothills of the Rockies and the lower portion of the great Alberta Plain, which ranges from semi-arid prairie to fertile farm and ranchland. American visitors to this part of Alberta will be reminded of their own West: the region is one of rolling grasslands bisected by streams and broken by rimrocks, cliffs and sandstone formations. In east-central Alberta are the Badlands, where softer rocks thrust up during the time of the dinosaurs were scoured by ice and erosion into deep ravines, exposing multi-colored layers of rock, and the characteristic hoodoos. These strangely named formations consist of alternate layers of rock and sandstone, in which the softer sandstone is eroded to create fantastically shaped columns sustained by the stronger rock cap. The Drumheller region is rich in dinosaur and other fossil remains, which can be viewed along the 48-kilometre circular Dinosaur Trail that begins in Drumheller. Along the way is the amazing new Tyrrell Museum of Paleontology in Midland Provincial Park—a $30 million facility that presents multi-media exhibits encompassing three billion years of life on earth. International scientific attention has been focused on the area since 1884, when Dr J B Tyrrell discovered the head of a petrified dinosaur here. Subsequent explorations unearthed some of the world's most significant fossils.

Midway between Calgary and Edmonton is the thriving city of Red Deer, whose Waskasoo Park is a much-frequented recreation center. Nearby Sylvan Lake, with its extensive beach, is a popular summer resort. West of here the scenic David Thompson Highway traverses farmlands and foothills on its way to the Saskatchewan River Crossing in Banff National Park.

West of Calgary is the wide-ranging Kananaskis Country Provincial Park, and to the south is lovely Waterton Lakes National Park. Nanton is located in some of Alberta's best ranchland and offers thirst-quenching spring water piped in from the Porcupine Hills and bottled for sale throughout the province. The east-west Crowsnest Highway passes through Lethbridge, Alberta's third largest city. Once a coal town, Lethbridge is now an irrigated oasis in the dry southern prairie. Throughout this region are reminders of its frontier heritage: whiskey-trading Fort Whoop-up, Indian Battle Park on the Oldman River, and the Fort Macleod Provincial Historic Site. Year-round sunshine and surprisingly high temperatures in winter bless the southwestern corner of Alberta. This is because the Chinook, a Pacific westerly wind, breathes its warmth on the region after releasing its moisture on the Continental Divide. The land of the Chinook also boasts fine hoodoo formations along the Milk River Valley, a classic badlands environment, now a provincial park, Writing-on-Stone. Fascinating native pictographs are inscribed on these rocks, revealing Alberta's prehistoric past.

99 The glow of sunset over the foothills west of High River competes with the rising full moon.

100-101 The massive rock formations at Burstall Pass in Kananaskis Country Provincial Park rise dramatically from the valley below.

102 The trails around Chester Lake, Kananaskis Provincial Park, lead avid hikers into the heart of Kananaskis country, with its thick spruce forests and rocky alpine meadows.

103 Mount Allan, site of the 1988 Winter Olympic Games, stands streaked with ski runs.

104-105 Cowboys round up cattle in the Porcupine Hills, south of Calgary.

106-107 The golden leaves of poplars in autumn draw a sunny canopy over young evergreens.

108 The TransCanada Highway winds its way
west to the Rocky Mountains through prairie and
foothill country.

109 Golden fields of wheat near Pincher Creek in southern Alberta gently sway in the warm wind.

110-111 A cattle drive in the vast prairie of southeastern Alberta evokes the pioneer spirit of this region.

112 *This watchful little cowboy is preparing for a future on the ranch.*

113 *Cowboys regroup on a cattle drive.*

*114–115 Brightly painted farmsteads and silos
in Queensland, southern Alberta, punctuate
the vast expanse of wheat fields.*

116-117 *Combines work relentlessly during the harvest to bring in the golden crops.*

117 *The plains of southern Alberta yield rich and abundant harvests of wheat, a major staple of Alberta's economy.*

118 *Picturesque McDougall Church stands peacefully in Stoney Indian Reserve, near Morley.*

119 *Elevators help move the grain into cargo trains, which then carry the precious load to the major distribution centres.*

120-121 *The haunting rock formations of Dinosaur Provincial Park cover some 90 square kilometres along the Red Deer River, and have some of the most extensive fossil remains in the world.*

122 *Alberta's Badlands are a region of dramatic crags and buttes rising from the prairie level.*

123 *An elk skull is an eerie reminder of the harshness of nature in the Badlands.*

124-125 *The Red Deer River snakes through the Badlands near Drumheller, a paleontological centre of international repute.*

126 The Prince of Wales Hotel attracts visitors to Waterton Lakes National park, on the border between Alberta and Montana, USA.

127 A peaceful sunset over Sylvan Lake, west of Red Deer.

128 Banff Springs Hotel, aglow in the evening light, beckons the tired traveller to a night of quiet and rest.